BIRDS
Around Us
by Marjorie Stuart
Illustrated by Waclav Perkowski

Prepared under the editorial direction of Dr. George Sutton, Research Professor of Zoology, Curator of Birds, The University of Oklahoma.

WHITMAN PUBLISHING COMPANY
Racine, Wisconsin

Contents

What Is a Bird?   9

Ancient Birds   10

Common Birds of North America   12

Some Interesting Facts   16

When the White Man Came   18

Eastern and Western Birds   20

Some Birds Stay   24

Some Birds Migrate   25

Information contained in the chart on page 49 is adapted from *An Introduction to Ornithology* by George Wallace. The author gratefully acknowledges the co-operation of Mr. Wallace and The Macmillan Company.

Library of Congress Catalog Card Number: 61-9973

Printed in the U.S.A.

Winter Birds   31

Birds Have Homesteads   32

Birds in Their Habitats   34

You Can Tell What They Eat   38

Eggs   40

Some Birds Make No Nest   42

Some Birds Build Skimpy Nests   43

Most Birds Build Sturdy Nests   44

Some Birds Nest in Holes   46

Some Birds Need Help   48

Birds Fly—Why Can't I?   50

How Birds See   52

What Makes a Bird so Light?   53

Feathers   54

Birds Are Always Hungry!   57

OSTRICH

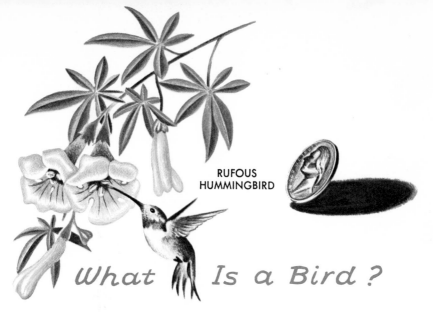

RUFOUS
HUMMINGBIRD

What Is a Bird?

Howold you know it's a bird? It's not because it can fly. Bats and insects fly, and not all birds do. But there is one sure way to tell that a creature is a bird. It's very simple: if it has feathers, it has to be a bird. No other animal wears feathers.

The biggest bird in the world, the ostrich, is eight feet tall and weighs three hundred pounds! It cannot fly at all, but runs swiftly on feet that have only two toes. Most birds have four-toed feet.

The hummingbird, the smallest bird, is also the world's most skillful flier. It can go up, down, backward, and even swing sideways in the air as if riding an invisible pendulum.

Hummingbirds are almost as small as bumblebees. Hold a nickel in your hand and feel how light it is. A ruby-throated hummingbird weighs less than that nickel!

Ancient Birds

Birds are descended from reptiles and still show this kinship by the scales on their feet and legs. The first birds lived 155 million years ago with the dinosaurs. The most ancient bird fossil known, archaeopteryx, was found in a slate quarry in Germany in 1861.

Archaeopteryx was about the size of our crow, had short, feathered wings with claws, and could fly. Like a lizard, it had a long tail supported by vertebrae. Unlike any lizard, it had feathers growing at the sides of its tail!

"Scarce as hen's teeth" is a good saying now, for today no bird has teeth. But archaeopteryx had thirty-two teeth set unevenly in a lizardlike beak!

ARCHAEOPTERYX
(Ar-kee-OP-ter-iks)
"ANCIENT WING"

In the area now known as Kansas, 120 million years ago there lived a large bird named ichthyornis. It was not very large, a gull-like bird. Scientists can tell by the breastbone and wing bones that this bird was a fine flier.

Hesperornis lived in Kansas at the same time. This "western bird," almost five feet long, could not fly. Its wings were too small.

At that time Kansas was covered by an inland sea. Hesperornis was a water bird which swam, dived, and caught fish for its food. Its feet were webbed and it had teeth.

ICHTHYORNIS
(Ik-thi-OR-nis)
"FISH BIRD"

HESPERORNIS
(Hes-per-OR-nis)
"WESTERN BIRD"

Common Birds of North America

THERE ARE OVER ONE THOUSAND kinds of birds in our country. They range in size from the California condor, with a wingspread of almost ten feet, to the calliope hummingbird, only three inches long.

AMERICAN GOLDFINCH

HOUSE WREN

BLUEBIRD

STARLING

ROBIN

CROW

KINGFISHER

BROWN
THRASHER

BLUE JAY

CARDINAL

MOURNING DOVE

ENGLISH SPARROW

How many of these common birds have you seen?

Some Interesting Facts

ALL BIRDS HAVE FEATHERS, two legs, two wings, and a bill. And they all hatch from eggs. But birds are not at all alike in their habits, in their body shapes, or in their colors.

The nighthawk flies over the heart of our busiest cities and sometimes raises a family on a city roof.

The California condor is upset when people come within a mile of his nest.

The mallard duck never gets wet. His feathers are waterproof.

The anhinga, or water

COMMON
NIGHTHAWK

CALIFORNIA
CONDOR

MALLARD
DUCK

WATER
TURKEY

**MALE
MOCKINGBIRD**

**CEDAR
WAXWING**

**MALE
PAINTED
BUNTING**

**FEMALE
PAINTED
BUNTING**

**GREAT
HORNED
OWL**

**EVERGLADES
KITE**

turkey, has to dry his feathers after every dive.

The male mockingbird can imitate any bird he hears. He can also sound just like a squeaky gate or a lost baby chicken.

The cedar waxwing is almost silent. He has only one lisping note.

The male painted bunting is our gaudiest American bird.

His mate is our only bird that looks like a plain green sparrow.

The great horned owl, found all over this country, eats mice, rabbits, skunks, and many other mammals.

The Everglades kite, or snail kite, dines only on one species of snail. The only snail kites in the United States live in southern Florida and are almost extinct.

When the White Man Came

Some birds were killed.

Passenger pigeons and Carolina parakeets were plentiful when America was discovered—but were killed in such numbers that they are now extinct.

Carolina parakeets roamed in great flocks over our eastern woodlands. They were about twice the size of the little cage parakeets we have now. When the flock came to a river-bank to drink, the ground seemed to be covered with a lush carpet of rich green, orange, and yellow. The birds ate seeds of pines and other trees. They even split open the prickly seed pods of the cocklebur with their strong curved bills.

The pioneers came, planted fruit trees and corn—and the parakeets flocked to the feast. They especially liked apple and pear seeds. When the farmers saw their food being eaten by birds, it is not surprising that they were indignant. If the Carolina parakeet had not enjoyed man's crops so much, we might still have this lovely bird.

The CAROLINA PARAKEET
looked like this.

Some birds were helped.

Robins moved across the country as men made clearings in the forests. Their heavy mud-lined nests needed solid support and the birds found many little "shelves" on the buildings man made. Robins can be found nesting today even in cities.

ROBIN

Chimney swifts nested in hollow trees and in caves before people came to build houses. Chimneys were a perfect substitute for natural nesting sites and were much more plentiful. The birds soon learned to use them.

Almost all purple martins now depend on man to furnish houses. Indians in the South hung large, dry gourds for the birds to nest in. Many rural people still have colonies of these lovely birds housed in gourds. Many "apartment houses" are put up for the martins.

CHIMNEY SWIFT

PURPLE MARTIN

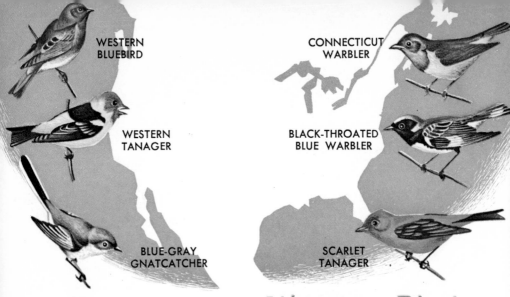

WESTERN BLUEBIRD

CONNECTICUT WARBLER

WESTERN TANAGER

BLACK-THROATED BLUE WARBLER

BLUE-GRAY GNATCATCHER

SCARLET TANAGER

Eastern and Western Birds

Birds in north america may be divided into eastern birds and western birds. They are alike, yet they are different. There is a very good reason for this. Birds migrate mostly north and south. They don't go east and west very often.

Tree-loving birds of the eastern states find the central Great Plains hard to cross. As there aren't many trees, the birds can't find a place where they are comfortable. The Rocky Mountains are a barrier for some birds, and the dry deserts stop others from finding new homes.

Many birds have, through the centuries, developed into eastern and western forms that look alike in some ways but not in others. Of these, one of the most interesting and easy to see is the flicker. This large woodpecker often comes to feeders and looks much the same from coast to coast except for one thing: the color under the wings and tail.

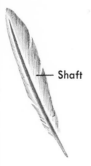

Shaft

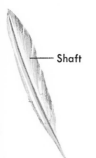

Shaft

The western bird is known as the red-shafted flicker because of the scarlet lining under wings and tail. The color is made by feathers with red shafts. A shaft could be called the backbone of a feather.

The eastern bird is called the yellow-shafted flicker because of the yellow underside of the wings and tail. In flight the wings and tail flash golden underneath.

Flickers have very long sticky tongues to capture the ants they like to eat. The tongue may be almost twice as long as the bird's head!

RED-SHAFTED
FLICKER

YELLOW-SHAFTED
FLICKER

RED-SHAFTED
FLICKER

21

BULLOCK'S
ORIOLE

WESTERN
KINGBIRD

AUDUBON'S
WARBLER

Bullock's oriole lives all over the western United States except high in the mountains. The female builds a strong, hanging nest of horsehair and fibers, then lines it with soft wool or down. The nest is often in a cottonwood or weeping willow tree, near a house.

The western kingbird is a bird of the open country. High on a telephone wire or treetop it watches for unwary insects. More colorful than the eastern kingbird, this bird has underparts of a pretty yellow. The nest is sometimes built on the crossbars of a telephone pole.

Audubon's warbler looks much like the eastern myrtle warbler, but has a bright yellow throat instead of white.

The male Baltimore oriole, brilliant in tropical colors of black and fiery orange, is one of the most familiar singers of the East. Like her western cousin, the female builds a long, hanging nest at the end of a drooping branch.

The eastern kingbird is gray and has a black tail clearly tipped with white. Kingbirds protect their nests by driving away crows or hawks much bigger than themselves.

The myrtle warbler comes to feeders and sometimes stays in southern states all winter. This bird has four spots of yellow in its plumage: one on the crown, one on the rump, one on each side of the chest.

MALE
BALTIMORE
ORIOLE

EASTERN
KINGBIRD

MYRTLE
WARBLER

23

BOBWHITE
QUAIL

CHICKADEE

Some Birds Stay

Cʜɪᴄᴋᴀᴅᴇᴇꜱ, ᴄᴀʀᴅɪɴᴀʟꜱ, ǫᴜᴀɪʟ, and many woodpeckers stay near the same place all year round. Many a bobwhite quail never in his life goes more than a half mile from the place where he was hatched.

Chickadees roam the woods in winter in little flocks with kinglets, nuthatches, brown creepers, and maybe a downy woodpecker. Flitting from tree to tree, they peer into crevices of bark and along leafless branches for insect eggs and chilled insects.

Chickadees usually find a soft, dead stub of a branch in the spring and dig out a nesting hole with their small bills. Sometimes they use a hole already made and discarded by a woodpecker.

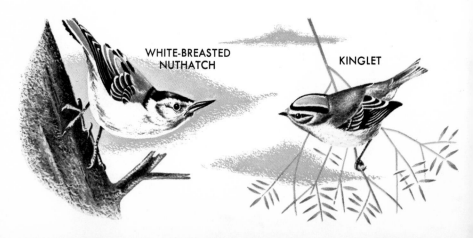

WHITE-BREASTED
NUTHATCH

KINGLET

Some Birds Migrate

BIRDS THAT STAY IN ONE PLACE all their lives are the exception, not the rule. Most birds have two homes—one for winter, one for summer. This movement between homes is called migration.

The homing ability of birds is amazing. By banding birds, scientists have proved that individuals of many species annually return to the same place to build their nests. Flickers and bluebirds will return to the same nesting box year after year.

BLUEBIRD

Scientists fasten bands around the legs of birds. Stamped on the bands is information which other scientists find helpful. The migration habits of birds are often discovered in this way.

Migrating birds follow the same routes year after year. Golden plovers, which nest in eastern parts of Arctic America, fly across a great stretch of the Atlantic Ocean to reach their winter homes in South America. When they return north in the spring, they fly through the interior rather than across the ocean or along the coast. The golden plovers which nest in western Alaska fly southward across the Pacific Ocean to their winter homes on faraway islands.

How do birds tell directions so accurately? Scientists are not sure. A bird's sense of direction is a great unsolved mystery.

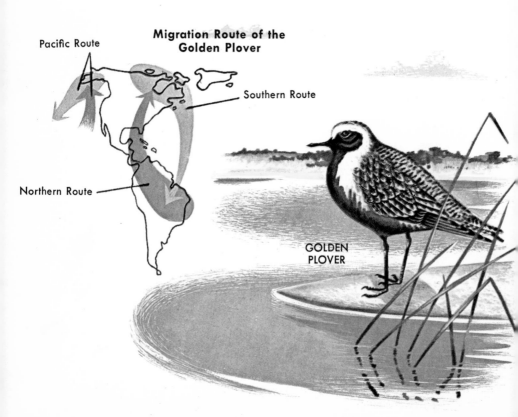

Pacific Route

Migration Route of the Golden Plover

Southern Route

Northern Route

GOLDEN PLOVER

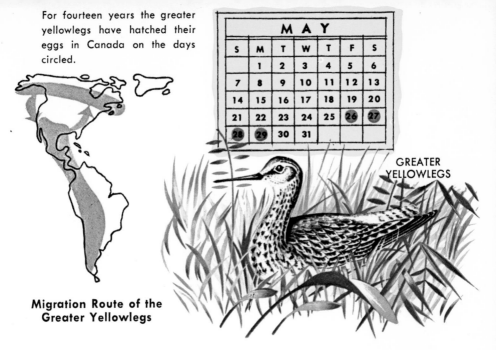

For fourteen years the greater yellowlegs have hatched their eggs in Canada on the days circled.

M A Y

S	M	T	W	T	F	S
	1	2	3	4	5	6
7	8	9	10	11	12	13
14	15	16	17	18	19	20
21	22	23	24	25	26	27
28	29	30	31			

GREATER
YELLOWLEGS

Migration Route of the Greater Yellowlegs

Birds don't wait for cold weather to tell them it is time to go south. Many move southward long before their food gets scarce. And in the spring, they know when to start back to their nesting grounds—local weather conditions have little to do with it.

Days get shorter in the fall, longer in the spring. For each kind of bird, there is a certain day-length that starts migration.

The timing of migration is so exact that for fourteen years the greater yellowlegs, long-legged shore birds, have hatched their earliest eggs between May 26 and May 29 in wild parts of Canada. And this is after a migration trip of from eight to ten thousand miles from Patagonia, in southern Argentina!

GEESE

Canadian geese are among the earliest to fly north in the spring. They travel in long V's with an old, experienced gander leading the flock. Their honking can be heard as they fly overhead, day or night.

Most birds travel at night and feed and rest in the daytime. Ducks, geese, cranes, and shore birds travel both day and night. Swallows, however, feed as they travel and probably migrate only during the day. Migrating swallows sometimes continue to pass over a pond or meadow all day long, as if the supply of swallows would never run out!

SWALLOWS

Some birds make short migration trips.

Birds that eat seeds and winter fruits can find food close to their nesting grounds.

Robins stay in the United States. All winter long they wander the sheltered valleys of the South. Horned larks and meadow larks seldom go far from their nesting grounds.

HORNED
LARK

MEADOW
LARK

During the nesting season the meadow lark perches on a post or, perhaps, a telephone pole and sings his loud, sweet song. Meadow larks fly with regular wing beats and then glide with stiff, outstretched wings. No other bird flies in quite this way.

Meadow larks build cleverly concealed nests on the ground. Even where the grass is short, the nest is covered with an arch of grass and weed stems and is hard to find. Only if the female flies out will one find this dainty grass nest with five white eggs speckled with brown and purple.

Meadow Lark
Nest

CHIMNEY SWIFT

Some birds make long migration trips.

Birds that live on insects must go far south to find food.

The champion traveler of the land birds is probably the nighthawk. This bird nests north to the Yukon and winters seven thousand miles to the south, in Argentina.

Purple martins and barn swallows winter in Brazil.

Chimney swifts spend the winter in Peru. In spring they fly back to the United States and southern Canada where they nest in chimneys. They look like flying cigars as they twitter overhead. Swifts fly very fast and dodge and dart about, catching the insects that are their only food.

Their nests are little saucer halves made of dead twigs glued together with saliva. Swifts never perch, so they must gather twigs as they fly. If you watch closely, you may see the birds break twigs from branches with their feet.

WINTER
GOLDFINCH

SUMMER
GOLDFINCH

Winter Birds

Some birds change color with the seasons. In summer the male goldfinch is bright yellow with black cap, wings, and tail. But the black cap and yellow body plumage are replaced by brown in winter. The male cardinal, on the other hand, stays bright red all year.

Tree sparrows are found in the United States only in winter. In spring they fly north to the very edge of the arctic barrens where they nest.

The junco is a well-known winter bird. There are several kinds of juncos, but all of them have white outer tail feathers. They nest in Canada and Alaska and also in the Appalachian Mountains as far south as West Virginia and North Carolina. The one found throughout the eastern United States in winter is called the slate-colored junco.

TREE SPARROW

SLATE-COLORED
JUNCO

Birds Have Homesteads

MALE ORIOLES, ROBINS, RED-WINGED BLACKBIRDS, and rose-breasted grosbeaks fly north before the females do. Each male must pick out a place to raise his family. He sings loudly and displays his bright spring plumage to serve notice on others of his kind that this homestead is taken. A bird's homestead is called his territory.

House wrens are content with a small yard. Robins need a big yard. Great horned owls claim a square mile of hunting territory. Other birds may nest in a territory, but each bird fights off birds of its own kind.

CARDINAL

A cardinal may spy his reflection in a window, fly at it with cries of rage and strike at the glass with beak and sharp claws. When the reflection fails to go away, the cardinal may move to a spot less full of "stubborn cardinals." His mate will fight her reflection, too. She is just as opposed to a rival female as a male is to a rival male.

Birds must claim territories in order to have space enough to find food for their hungry youngsters. It's always mealtime for nestlings!

There is nothing as hungry as a baby bird. The parents poke food deep into the baby's throat so it can swallow. The noisiest baby gets the most food.

MARSH WREN

One pair of house wrens made 1,217 trips to the nest with food in one day. Once a robin just ready to leave the nest was fed all the earthworms he could eat. He ate fourteen *feet* of earthworms in one day!

Baby birds eat mostly insects. Even seed-eating birds such as cardinals raise their babies on insects.

Weevil

Larva

Black Swallowtail or Parsley Caterpillar

But they eat other things too:

Spider

Earthworm

Crayfish

Red-tailed hawks catch snakes to feed their husky nestlings. And barn owls give their babies mice and cotton rats.

Birds in Their Habitats

RED-EYED
VIREO

WHITE-BREASTED
NUTHATCH

TOWHEE

DOWNY
WOODPECKER

SOME BIRDS LIVE IN PLACES where there are lots of trees and shrubs. Many of these birds patrol our woods and forests and eat the insect pests.

The red-eyed vireo is one of the commonest birds in America. But vireos are hard to see. They feed high in the treetops where their greenish colors blend in with the leaves. This one can be located by listening for his song. The male sings all day long all summer.

The white-breasted nuthatch goes down tree trunks head first, searching for tiny insects and their eggs.

The towhee can be heard in the underbrush as he shuffles around, kicking up dead leaves. He jumps up in the air and scratches in the forest litter with both feet at once!

The downy woodpecker is found everywhere in woodlands and often eats suet at feeders in winter. He is sparrow-sized and has a broad white line down his back. Notice how he uses his tail as a prop.

HORNED
LARK

Some birds live in open places.

Wherever there is an airport or other large area of short grass, the horned lark is apt to be walking around policing the ground for insects. Some birds hop. This one walks. The horned lark is found all over North America.

The road runner, found in the southwestern United States, has long, strong legs. He dodges recklessly among the cactuses after the swift lizards he eats. He also likes snakes, scorpions, tarantulas, centipedes, and grasshoppers.

Motionless and alone on a wire or in the top of a tree, the loggerhead shrike watches and waits for his prey. His eyesight is so amazing that he sees insects at great distances and flies right to them! He flies low above the ground and glides sharply upward to his perch. If he is not extra hungry he fastens his prey to a thorn. This habit gives him the nickname "butcher bird."

ROAD
RUNNER

LOGGERHEAD
SHRIKE

Some birds live in or near water.

White pelicans herd fish into the shallows and scoop them up with huge bills that have built-in shopping baskets underneath. Brown pelicans dive for fish from the air. Pelicans have webbed feet for swimming.

The great blue heron stands motionless, posed like a statue at the edge of the water.

The shoveler is a duck with an oddly shaped bill. He strains food from shallow water.

You may think the pied-billed grebe has drowned when he dives. He comes up hundreds of feet away.

An osprey catches fish with his strong-taloned feet.

PIED-BILLED
GREBE

PELICAN

GREAT
BLUE
HERON

KILLDEER

SPOTTED
SANDPIPER

Red-winged blackbirds build their nests in cattails by the edge of water. The mother red-wing is a streaked, brownish bird that doesn't look related to her glossy mate.

The coot is found in ponds, lakes, and open water. This is the only swimming bird that looks black with a white bill. The side flaps on his green toes help him swim.

The spotted sandpiper teeters all his life except when he is asleep.

The killdeer is a noisy bird who calls his own name and has two dark bands across his chest.

37

You Can Tell What They Eat

The shape of a bird's bill and feet will tell you what it eats or how it gets food.

Sparrows have strong short bills to crush seeds and sturdy feet to hop on.

SPARROW

HAWK

Hawks have hooked bills and taloned feet to capture rats, rabbits, and field mice.

Nighthawks are insect eaters. They fly around with big mouths wide open to scoop up insects on the wing. Their bills are small and their feet are weak.

NIGHTHAWK

Herons have long bills, long necks, and long legs and toes so that they can wade out in the water and catch fish.

Woodpeckers have strong bills to chisel through wood. They hold themselves up with their X-shaped feet and

TRICOLORED HERON

short stiff tail feathers. Their long barbed tongues help them capture grubs deep in their burrows.

WOODPECKER

HUMMINGBIRD

Hummingbirds have long slim bills. Their tongues are hollow, like two drinking straws side by side, for drinking nectar from deep within flowers. The tongues are sticky, too, for catching tiny insects. Their feet are too weak to walk on, but hummingbirds fly so well they don't need to walk. They seem to "stand on air" in front of a blossom and their wings beat so fast that they are almost invisible.

Snipes have slim bills for probing. With the tips of their bills, these birds can feel their food deep in the mud. They have long toes to support them on soft mud.

SNIPE

39

Eggs

BOBWHITE

Until two hundred years ago the elephant bird, which stood ten feet tall, lived on Madagascar, an island near Africa. This bird laid the largest egg ever known. It was bigger than a football and held two gallons—as much as 148 hen's eggs or thirty thousand hummingbird's eggs!

All female birds lay eggs and the eggs must be kept warm until they hatch. All baby birds need care.

Most shore birds nest on the ground and lay big eggs for their size. Their babies stay in the egg a long time and are ready to run and hunt food as soon as their downy coat has dried.

The coot, killdeer, spotted sandpiper, quail, and duck all have babies that leave the nest to follow their mother soon after hatching. It takes twenty-six days for a killdeer egg to hatch.

Tufted Duck
Three Fourths Actual Size

Killdeer
One Half
Actual Size

Spotted Sandpiper
One Half
Actual Size

Wren
Actual Size

Arizona Woodpecker
Actual Size

Chimney Swift
Actual Size

Many birds lay small eggs that hatch in fourteen days or less. Their babies are practically naked and very helpless. Wrens, robins, woodpeckers, chimney swifts, and chickadees all have helpless young. Nests are the nurseries these birds build so their babies can grow up safely.

Robin
One Half Actual Size

The egg begins
to crack.

At last the baby
robin frees itself.

When a baby bird is ready to come out of the shell, it chips its way out with the only tooth a bird ever has. The bill, which is soft at this stage, has a hard little lump on the end of it called the "egg tooth." It disappears soon after the little bird has hatched.

Quail
One Half Actual Size

Horned Lark
Actual Size

Coot
Three Fourths Actual Size

KILLDEER

Some Birds Make No Nest

RED-EYED VIREO

THE KILLDEER IS TYPICAL of the many birds that lay their eggs on bare sand or dirt. The eggs are colored to blend with the surroundings. Killdeer parents are great actors! They often put on a "broken-wing" act to lure people away from their eggs. They are noisy, excitable birds who call, "Kill-dee, kill-dee!"

The nighthawk often lays her two splotchy eggs on bare graveled roofs in cities.

The cowbird baby is on the left.

The cowbird lays her egg in the nest of some other bird and the foster parents hatch and care for the little cowbird. Often this baby is bigger than the "parent"; it is a comical sight to see a red-eyed vireo feeding a youngster nearly twice the vireo's size!

Some Birds Build Skimpy Nests

THE MOURNING DOVE'S TWO WHITE EGGS can often be seen through the bottom of the loosely made twig nest. At times this bird nests on the ground with only a few twigs scattered around the eggs.

Herons and egrets, which nest in colonies called rookeries, build coarse platforms of sticks and twigs. Several of these big nests may be in the same tree.

The coot builds a simple platform of water plants and anchors it to tall reeds.

The pied-billed grebe builds a floating nest. When the female leaves her eggs she covers them with wet, dead cattail leaves.

Mourning Dove
Nest

Coot Nest

Grebe
on Her Nest

Most Birds Build Sturdy Nests

Eᴀᴄʜ ʙɪʀᴅ ʜᴀꜱ ᴀ ꜱᴘᴇᴄɪᴀʟ ᴋɪɴᴅ ᴏꜰ ɴᴇꜱᴛ and is born knowing how to build it. Once a robin was raised by a scientist and never saw a nest. Yet when the time came, she built a nest of mud and grass just like a robin raised in the wild!

ROBIN

Barn swallows build their nests of mud, lined with feathers, under rafters in barns. Now that barns are becoming scarce, these swallows often nest in culverts under our highways. You can always recognize a barn swallow by its deeply forked tail.

The ruby-throated hummingbird builds a dainty nest of bud scales and spider webs. It covers the outside with lichens to look like the wood around it. You can hardly tell this tiny nest from a knot on the branch.

BARN
SWALLOW

RUBY-THROATED
HUMMINGBIRD

44

RED-EYED
VIREO

AMERICAN
GOLDFINCH

YELLOW
WARBLER

The red-eyed vireo builds a durable hanging nest of bark and fiber bound together with spider webs. Most birds are quiet around their nests, but this one sings even while he's carrying food to his nestlings.

The goldfinch makes a beautiful nest of fine grasses lined with thistledown. Goldfinches don't start nesting until late summer when thistles have seeded and they have plenty of food for their broods. They eat the seeds themselves, then bring up the partly digested food for their young.

A yellow warbler will often add a second story to its thick-walled grass-and-plant-fiber nest to bury a cowbird egg. It seems strange that they don't just jab the egg and throw it out, but their bills may not be strong enough to do this.

KINGFISHER

BANK SWALLOW

Some Birds Nest in Holes

THE KINGFISHER DIGS A LONG TUNNEL in the bank of a river or creek and makes a little room at the end. Here five or more white eggs are laid and hatched. The babies are fed on little fish.

Bank swallows gather in colonies that may number five hundred families. They dig tunnels in a vertical bank and put their feather-lined nests at the ends of the tunnels. Sometimes there are so many that the bank looks as if it were honeycombed with holes. These swallows can often be seen by the hundreds perched on wires near their nesting bank.

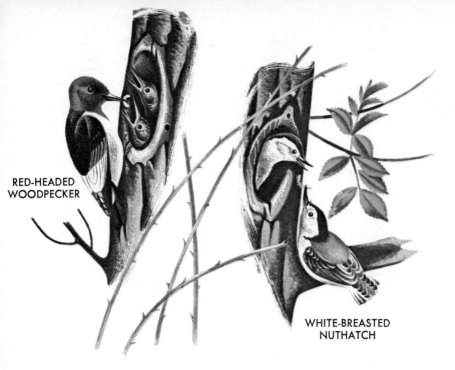

RED-HEADED
WOODPECKER

WHITE-BREASTED
NUTHATCH

The brilliantly colored red-headed woodpecker carves out a nesting hole in a high dead branch or even in a telephone pole. All woodpeckers have white eggs. Their babies grow up in a hole which has no lining except a few chips of wood. Red-headed woodpeckers like to live in open places where there are only a few trees. They often nest in towns and even in cities.

The white-breasted nuthatch likes to find a natural cavity in a tree trunk, but will use the discarded home of a woodpecker if necessary. The father bird feeds the mother while she stays on the nest to keep their freckled eggs warm. Nuthatches line their nest holes with a warm soft bed of moss, fur, and feathers.

Martin House

Wren House

Some Birds Need Help

Many birds that nest in holes must find the holes already made. These are the birds we can help by building birdhouses.

First decide which of your local hole-nesting birds you would like to help. Then make the house in the size the bird needs, fasten it up safely, and leave it for the birds to find. It doesn't have to be fancy. Birds seem to like plain houses best.

BLUEBIRD

Bird

House Wren

Bluebird

Screech Owl

Flicker

Purple Martin
(each apartment)

The entrance hole for a house wren should be shaped like a diamond and just this size. A hole this shape keeps English sparrows out and lets the wrens get twigs inside.

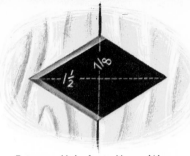

Entrance Hole for a House Wren

Purple martins like to nest in a house that holds several martin families. A martin house should be placed on a pole, well above ground, in an open spot.

Birds have to find nesting material. People often put out string or yarn for orioles. Robins use mud and will take it from a pan. A container of coarse wire mesh stuffed with feathers and cotton attracts many birds.

Notice to Birdhouse Builders: Use These Measurements.

Size of Floor (inches)	Height (inches)	Entrance Above Floor (inches)	Diameter of Hole (inches)	Height Above Ground (feet)
4 x 4	6	4	⅞ x 1½	6–10
5 x 5	8	6	1½	5–10
9 x 9	15	12	3¼	10–30
7 x 7	18	15	2½	6–20
6 x 6	6	1	2½	15–20

Birds Fly –
Why Can't I ?

A BIRD'S WINGS MOVE VERY QUICKLY and steadily while it is flying. Try swinging your arms at a rate of one hundred to five hundred times a minute and you will have some idea of the power it takes for a bird to fly. To lift your weight, your arms, if they were wings, would each have to be more than fifty feet long!

We don't have muscles enough to fly even if we had wings. Birds have huge muscles to move their wings. Sometimes a third or more of the total weight of a bird is made up of these flying muscles! Flying birds all have breastbones shaped like the keel of a boat with space for attaching the muscles.

Compare the bone structure of a bird with the keel of a boat.

KEEL

Air pressure is the secret of flight.

Air flows above a bird's wing . . .

and below it. The bird is lifted by strong pressure of the air beneath its wings.

Birds are streamlined, so their bodies slip through the air like an airplane. In fact, a bird's wing is shaped like an airplane wing. As the bird flies forward, the rounded front edge of the wing forces air up. This air has to travel faster than the air that goes under the wing. The fast air above exerts less pressure on the top of the wing than the slow air below which pushes up.

In summer when hot air is rising, a vulture can glide in circles for hours without moving his wings enough for us to see. The rising air pushes up almost as hard as the weight pushes down and the bird glides "downhill" through the rising air.

Geese, good fliers, have long wings.

CANADA GOOSE

GAMBEL'S QUAIL

Quail, poor fliers, have stubby wings.

How Birds See

THE KEENEST OF A BIRD'S SENSES IS ITS SIGHT.

A sparrow hawk can see a grasshopper eight times as far away as a man can. In dim light a barn owl can see ten times as well as a human.

Some large hawks and owls, weighing only five pounds or so, have eyes just as big as the eyes of a full-grown human who may weigh 180 pounds!

We use two eyes and have "binocular" vision. This means that we see the same thing with both eyes. Owls see this way, too, for their eyes are set in front. But most birds have "monocular" vision. They see two separate pictures with eyes that are set at the sides of their heads. Most birds can see backwards as well as forwards. Watch how a sparrow cocks its head to focus one eye on a bit of grain before eating it.

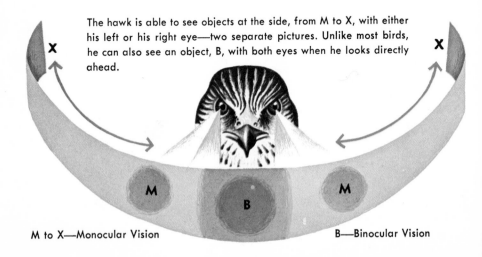

The hawk is able to see objects at the side, from M to X, with either his left or his right eye—two separate pictures. Unlike most birds, he can also see an object, B, with both eyes when he looks directly ahead.

M to X—Monocular Vision   B—Binocular Vision

CATBIRD

What Makes A Bird So light ?

A LOT OF A BIRD'S BULK is made up of feathers. Feathers are light and fluffy and the thicker parts are either hollow or filled with light pith.

A bird's body is lighter than it looks because a bird is full of air. Many of its bones are hollow and air-filled. We have lungs that are light and air-filled, but a bird has other air spaces besides lungs. There are a lot of air sacs, like balloons, inside a bird. These connect with the lungs and with the hollow bones.

In the summer when you see a bird panting with its bill open, it is probably trying to cool off. Birds have no sweat glands in the skin as we do. They get rid of extra heat by breathing rapidly. This carries moisture out of the air sacs.

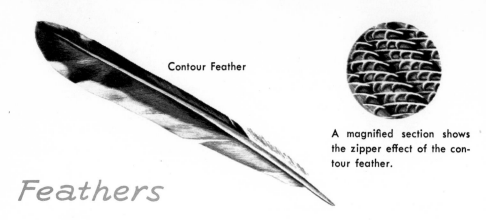

Contour Feather

A magnified section shows the zipper effect of the contour feather.

Feathers

Birds have two main kinds of feathers, contour feathers and down feathers.

Contour feathers cover most of the body to streamline it and to act as a protective covering. They give the bird a distinctive coloring. No other vertebrate is as variously colored as the bird.

A contour feather looks simple, but isn't. From the stiff central quill, barbs like little feathers extend outward. On them are many tiny barbs that lock together like a zipper. Often when you see a bird preening, pulling feathers through its beak, it is putting the "zippers" back in place to hold the loose fluffy parts of the feather firmly together.

Down feathers are soft and fluffy and have no zippers. They make a soft warm undercoating close to the bird's skin. Ducks and geese have lots of down feathers.

A hummingbird has fewer than one thousand feathers. A robin has nearly three thousand. A coot has almost fourteen thousand feathers!

Birds recognize each other by colors and markings. Egrets and herons have special feathers for spring when they need to look their best at courting time. Most birds wear their brightest, freshest colors in the springtime. Males are usually brighter than females.

EGRET

SPARROW

The most important use of feathers is to hold in body heat. Even in sub-zero weather a bird's body must be kept as hot as on a summer day. Feathers are like a blanket wrapped around the bird to keep it cozy and warm. In winter, just as we wear more clothes, some birds have more feathers. A goldfinch in winter has almost one thousand more feathers than in summer.

SPARROW

Birds are much hotter inside than any other creature. If your body were as hot as a bird's, you would feel very ill. People have inner regulators that keep their bodies at about ninety-eight degrees Fahrenheit—but many birds feel most comfortable when their bodies are at 110 degrees.

Just as food cooks faster over a hot flame than over a low one, this extra heat speeds up all of the things that a bird does. Your heart beats about seventy-two times a minute, but a sleeping chickadee has a heart beat of five hundred times a minute. Awake and frightened, its heart beats twice that fast.

In cold weather a sleeping bird often tucks its bill under a wing or deep in feathers. The air is warmer close to the bird's body, so tucking the bill under feathers is the only way a bird can breathe warm air and keep from chilling all of its insides.

A bird in winter sometimes looks very fat because of fluffed up feathers. Special muscles in the skin, like the ones that give us goose pimples, make the feathers stand up. This thicker covering, with all of its dead air space, is just like an extra blanket.

ROBIN

Birds Are Always Hungry

A BIRD'S FOOD DIGESTS SO QUICKLY that it spends most of its life looking for something to eat. Often food goes completely through a bird's digestive tract in one and a half hours!

If you ate as much as a hummingbird, you might eat twice your weight in sugar syrup every day and top it off with a tasty twenty or thirty pounds of soft insects!

Chimney swift babies eat their own weight in insects every day. The parents spend nearly all the daylight hours on the wing searching for food. A family of swifts may eat as many as ten thousand insects in one day!

In the winter most wild birds have lots of fat on them. The fat is stored nourishment which keeps them alive in cold weather. Even this cannot keep them alive when ice or snow hide all their food. A bird can starve to death if there are two very cold days in a row when it cannot find food or when the food is covered with ice. A bird needs a lot to eat just to keep warm.

Feeders in our yards bring lots of birds close enough for us to see them easily. A shelf on a post makes a good feeder. Grain can be scattered on the ground.

You can be a real friend to the birds in winter by putting out food for them. But *don't* start feeding in the fall unless you plan to keep it up all winter. When birds have learned to depend upon you, two days of no food on the feeder can mean starvation for them.

A favorite food of birds is suet, beef fat. Butchers often give it away. If it is ground, blue jays can't carry off huge chunks.

Sunflower seeds, squash seeds, and almost any kind of nuts attract birds. The "scratch feed" that farmers buy for chickens is a wonderful food for our native sparrows and other ground feeders. Many birds are fond of peanut butter.

Hummingbirds will sip sugar syrup from little bottles decorated to look like flowers. They sometimes become very tame.

RUBY-THROATED
HUMMINGBIRD

Summer and winter, a favorite food of birds is this mush:

Mix:
2 cups of yellow corn meal
2 cups of sugar
2 cups of ground suet
1 cup of flour
Add 2 cups of water and cook about five minutes.
Stir while cooking, as mush burns easily.

Keep the mush in the refrigerator and put some out fresh each day.

Blue jays, orioles, mockingbirds, cardinals, robins, wrens, and many other birds love this mush. The red-headed woodpecker often brings his dark-headed youngsters to perch on the edge of the shelf while he feeds them mush.

Birds need water, too. They love to fly through the spray of a sprinkler. They will drink and bathe in a shallow pan of water. They enjoy bathing even in cold weather. Wait until you see a whole flock of cedar waxwings bathing together!

RED-HEADED
WOODPECKER

WHAT IS MOON MILK?

HOW DO ENGINES WORK?

HOW DEEP CAN DIVERS GO?

Whitman
Learn About Books

BUTTERFLIES, SKIPPERS, AND MOTHS
James S. Ayars and Milton W. Sanderson

INSECTS, LITTLE WONDERS OF THE WORLD
Robert N. Webb

REPTILES, SINCE THE WORLD BEGAN
Ben Bova

ANIMALS OF THE JUNGLE
Robert N. Webb

THE SEA AND ITS WONDERFUL CREATURES
Ronald Rood

ANIMALS OF LONG AGO
Raymond Jones

**THE MICROSCOPE
AND A HIDDEN WORLD TO EXPLORE**
Irene S. Pyszkowski

ASTRONOMY—OUR SOLAR SYSTEM AND BEYOND
Robert I. Johnson

ADVENTURES IN SCIENCE
Charles D. Neal

ROCKETS TO EXPLORE THE UNKNOWN
Don E. Rogers

FIND OUT! FIRST STEP TO THE FUTURE
Dr. Dan Q. Posin

Whitman
REG. U.S. PAT. OFF.

BOOKS IN THE LEARN ABOUT SERIES

THE AIRPORT, OUR LINK TO THE SKY
Robert Sidney Bowen

ANIMALS OF THE FIELD AND FOREST
Mina Lewiton

BIRDS AROUND US
Marjorie Stuart

FLOWERS AND WHAT THEY ARE
Mary Elting

TREES AND HOW THEY GROW
Katharine Carter

OUR EARTH, WHAT IT IS
Frederick H. Pough

ROCKS AND WHAT THEY TELL US
Lester del Rey

RIVERS, WHAT THEY DO
Nancy Larrick and Alexander Crosby

PHYSICS, ITS MARVELS AND MYSTERIES
Dr. Daniel Q. Posin

THE BIG BUILDERS
E. Joseph Dreany

TURN TO THE SEA
Athelstan Spilhaus

CAVES AND THEIR MYSTERIES
James McClurg

ENGINES, PROGRESS AND POWER
Don E. Rogers

YOUR BODY
Harry Swartz, M.D